1

4

7

INSIDE THE BONE MARROW...

WELCOME TO THE BONE MARROW, RICHARD. WHAT DO YOU THINK?

THIS IS AMAZING!

IT'S LIKE OUR DRAMA ROOM AT SCHOOL—ONLY BIGGER, BETTER AND FULL OF *DANCING BLOOD CELLS!*

WAIT A MINUTE... WE'RE *INSIDE* A BONE? WHAT DO BONES HAVE TO DO WITH BLOOD CELLS?

BONE MARROW IS A VITAL PART OF UNDERSTANDING LEUKAEMIA BECAUSE IT'S WHERE *BLOOD CELLS ARE BORN!*

14

15

THE DOCTOR NEEDS TO TAKE A SAMPLE OF YOUR BLOOD TO SEE IF YOU HAVE LEUKAEMIA. DOCTORS COUNT THE NUMBER OF **WEEDS, NORMAL DEFENDERS, TRANSPORTERS AND FIX-IT GUYS.**

NORMAL SAMPLE

PURPLE WEED CLUSTER

IF THE *WEED* COUNT IS *HIGH* AND THE *NORMAL DEFENDERS* COUNT IS *LOW,* THE DOCTOR WILL NEED TO DO ANOTHER TEST.

CLOSE UP OF WEEDS

THE DOCTOR NEEDS TO TAKE A SAMPLE OF THE MARROW GARDEN FROM INSIDE THE BONE. THIS IS CALLED A *BONE MARROW BIOPSY* OR *BONE MARROW ASPIRATE.* THIS IS THE *BEST* WAY TO TELL IF SOMEONE HAS LEUKAEMIA.

FOR MORE INFORMATION ON *BONE MARROW BIOPSY* OR *BONE MARROW ASPIRATE,* PLEASE GO TO MEDIKIDZ.COM

PURPLE WEEDS HAVE TAKEN OVER!

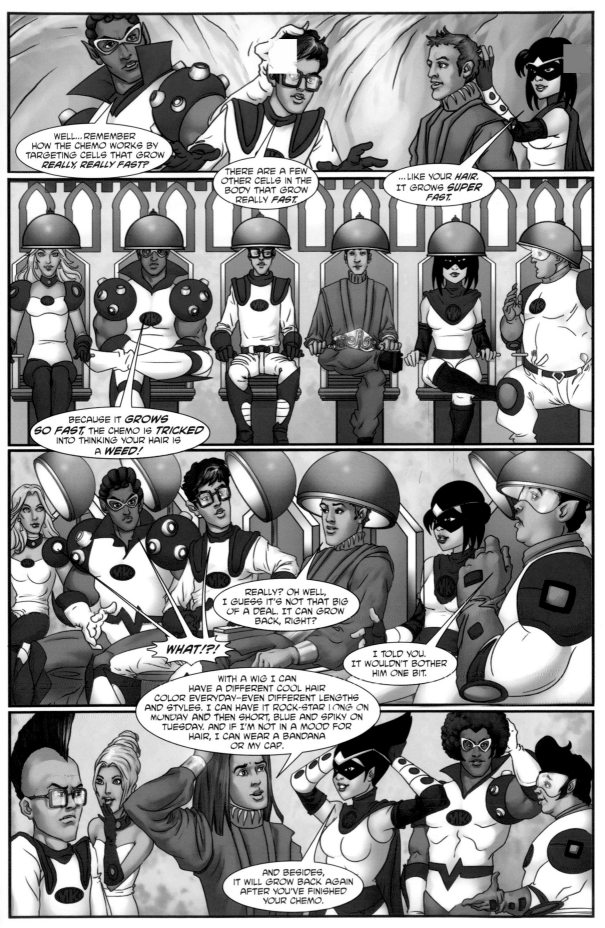

23

25

BACK INSIDE THE BONE MARROW...

WHAT'S HAPPENED HERE! IT USED TO BE... SO *BUSY*!

ALL THE WEEDS HAVE BEEN REMOVED BY THE CHEMO, THEN NEW SEEDS ARE PLANTED. THEY GROW UP TO BE *DEFENDERS*, *TRANSPORTERS* AND *FIX-IT GUYS–JUST LIKE NORMAL*!

SOMETIMES, IF THE CHEMO IS NOT ABLE TO KILL ALL THE WEEDS, THE BAD BONE MARROW CAN BE REPLACED BY SOMETHING CALLED A TRANSPLANT.

YOUR *CELLS BEHAVING BADLY* ARE SWAPPED WITH MAGIC SEEDS FROM SOMEONE ELSE.

THE PROPER MEDICAL TERM IS *BONE MARROW TRANSPLANT*.

THEN, THE NEW SEEDS GROW INTO *NORMAL BABY BLOOD CELLS* IN YOUR BONE MARROW GARDEN!

WOW! LOOK AT THEM GROW! THEY ARE SO WELL TRAINED!

AMAZING!

MOST CHILDREN DON'T NEED TO HAVE RADIOTHERAPY OR A BONE MARROW TRANSPLANT. IN MOST KIDS, THE CHEMO DOES THE TRICK ALL ON ITS OWN.

DOCTORS ARE NOT SURE WHY SOME PEOPLE DEVELOP LEUKAEMIA, BUT YOU'RE NOT IN THIS ALONE! YOUR FAMILY AND THE HOSPITAL STAFF ARE ON YOUR SIDE AND THEY'RE WORKING HARD TO HELP YOU!